Quotes on Depression and Suicide

Collected and Edited by

Dr. Krishna N. Sharma

Disclaimer: The editor or the publication do not own the rights of the quotes. The editor do not claim the quotes to be original and confirms that it has been collected from various resources

Copyright Free

All rights reserved.

ISBN: 1481069594
ISBN-13: 978-1481069595

"I do cut, and cry, and lie.

I don't cut...

I fell...

I would always tell you,

My dog bit me...

So don't even try."

These easy lies.

When you really didn't know,

You don't know me."

"A pill to make you numb, a pill to you make you dumb, a pill to make you anybody else, but all the drugs in this world won't save her from herself."

"And sometimes I have really bad day... when, you know, I just want to hide or scream or bleed or something..."

"How can you understand me when I can't understand myself?"

"Beware the person who has nothing to lose."

"Are you running away from something you don't want? Or running away from something you're afraid to want?"

"As long as you know everything is a lie then you can't hurt yourself."

"As she's breaking down she grabs her razor and she whispers... this time I'm not okay..."

"Be patient and tough; some day this pain will be useful to you."

"Behind this innocent smile of mine, lay words left unsaid. Words of longing, love, anger, and hate, all repeated inside my head."

"But it's ironic because that's how I live my life. I smile

on the outside, and everyone thinks I'm doing fine but I'm always dieing inside, always one step away from the edge you know? I can't be happy to be who I am because I don't know who I am anymore."

"But then I never had to worry about crash landing because I never took off."

"Crimson tears run down my arm, All the pain and all the harm. My only way to let it out, I wanna scream, I wanna shout. But I don't make a sound, I keep it inside. I wanna break out, but instead I hide. I sit in my room, and hide in my shell, the life that I'm living, my own private hell. The crimson tears, down my arm they run. I look down at my arm, what have I done?"

"Cutters are living proof that when the body is ravaged the soul cries out and when the soul is trampled upon, the body bleeds."

"Cutting doesn't solve anything or take the pain away, but for those few seconds everything is Okay..."

"Cutting is a stepping stone for me. All my life I have

been put through so much emotional pain and I've let myself just sit and drown in it. I can't physically or emotionally do it anymore. So I cut. It temporarily takes my pain away until I am able to remove myself from all feeling. I am detached from everything right now... I am numb."

"Death is God's way of saying you're fired. Suicide is human's way of saying you can't fire me, I quit."

"Depression is merely anger minus the enthusiasm. "

"Depression is such a strong emotion, its regret, fear, frustration, isolation, a choice, and sometimes even a form of protection."

"Did it surprise you that I am not who you thought I was? Did it surprise you to find that I don't exactly stand for what you thought I stood for all along? Did it surprise you to find that I'm not exactly how I played myself out to be? That the person you thought I was is actually nothing to what I am."

"Do you ever have one of those days where nothing really goes wrong but you feel like you hate the world and the smallest thing that happens can make you break down right there and cry?"

"Do you ever have those times you cry and you don't know why?"

"Do you ever lay in bed at night hoping you wake up in the emergency room and hear the words 'she's not going to make it?"

"Do you remember the days when you were a child and simply running outside made you happy? What happened to them?"

"Don't fall into the trap of pretending everything's fine when you know it isn't."

"Don't hold strong opinions about things you don't understand."

"Even the people who never frown eventually breakdown."

"Every night before I go to sleep I lie on my bed and

stare up at my blank walls. I try to imagine the future, but right now it's as blank as those walls. All I can see is a past that I barely recognize any more."

"Every so often I want to dig my fingernails underneath my skin and peel off the face everybody's so used to seeing me in. Every so often I want people to know that I'm not as okay as they think I am."

"Every word, another scar, Some people say I cut for attention, Attention is the last thing I want, I tell them I've got my reasons, But what they don't know is, They are the reason I cut, I walk the halls and people talk, Their harsh words cut in deep, Don't they know what they're doing, Every word they say is another scar on my wrist."

"Everybody knows that something's wrong but nobody knows what's going on."

"Everybody's searching for a hero. People need someone to look up to. I never found anyone who fulfilled my need... a lonely place to be, and so I learned to depend on me."

QUOTES ON DEPRESSION AND SUICIDE

"Everyone is asking me how I feel, how I am and truthly I feel numb. I can't feel anything and honestly I like it."

"Everyone sees who I appear to be but only a few know the real me, you only see what I choose to show there's so much behind my smile you just don't know."

"Everything that ever caused a tear to trickle down my cheek, I run away and hide from it. But now, everything is unwinding and finding its way back towards me. And I don't know what to do. I just know that pain I felt so long ago, it's hurting ten times more."

"First time I cut was just to feel the pain, Strange because I didn't feel a thing."

"Her sadness did not have that. It dripped slowly into her life without her noticing it, at least, not noticing it until it consumed her fully and smothered her with darkness."

"How can you hide from what never goes away?"

"I am not what I ought to be, not what I want to be, but I am thankful that I am better than I used to be..."

"I am sad but I'm laughing."

"I believe in whatever gets you through the night. Night is the hardest time to be alive. For me, anyway. It lasts so long, and four am knows all my secrets. Four am is when my dreams die."

"I bleed for you that's why I cut those simple scars are just deep thoughts."

"I can't get my wrists to bleed, just don't know why suicide appeals to me."

"I can't stop crying... I don't understand, and it's not the loud, screaming crying... it's just the tears continuously roll down my face, and I can't do anything to stop them."

"I cry then I cut, then I cry again, it never ends."

"I cut to prove to you that you are not the only one that can hurt me."

"I don't care that I don't care, but I do care maybe a

little bit about not caring about not caring - but maybe I do feel sorry for all the nice people whose efforts are wasted on a waste case like me."

"I don't know if I'm getting better or just used to the pain."

"I don't know what I want in life. I don't know what I want right now. All I know is that I'm hurting so much inside that it's eating me, and one day, there won't be any of me left."

"I don't necessarily want to be happy; I just want to stop feeling miserable."

"I don't want the world to see me, because I don't think that they'd understand."

"I guess for some people it's always a little easier to appreciate the rainy days instead of sunny days..."

"I guess there comes a point where you just have to stop trying because it hurts too much to hold on anymore."

"I hate what I have become to escape what I hated being."

"I have a tendency to hurt myself physically, when I'm hurting inside."

"I have no clue why I do what I do. It feels good to have cold metal press against my skin as my problems tear at my soul. The blood drips softly and I cry silently. No one will ever understand me except for other people like me."

"I have to cut because it's the only way I can smile."

"I just like playing games with people, I always hope there'll be someone smart enough to see through me but you're all so stupid."

"I just realized that were all a bunch of actresses and we've fooled everyone into believing that we're all okay... I'm just waiting for the day when I can convince myself of that."

"I know it seems like I'm this strong person who can get though anything, but inside I'm fragile. I've had so many things thrown at me, and each one has only made a crack. What I'm afraid of is shattering."

"I know what it's like to want to die; how it hurts to smile; how you try to fit in but you can't; how you hurt yourself on the outside; to try to kill the thing that's in the inside."

"I like having low self-esteem it makes me feel special."

"I love sleep. My life has this tendency to fall apart when I'm awake."

"I never knew that one singe blade could mess up my life..."

"I only smile in the dark."

"I quit, I give up, nothing's good enough for anybody else, it see... when I am all alone its best way to be. When I'm by myself nobody else can say good-bye. Everything is temporary anyway."

"I smile, I smile all the time, you're just not around to

see it."

"I take the blade and run it gently against my skin, it cuts in deeper and deeper, the blood bursts out and slowly runs down my arm then it stops and the pain goes away."

"I used to have many faults, not I have only two - everything I say and everything I do..."

"I want to be remembered as the girl who always smiled the one who could brighten up your day, even if she couldn't brighten her own."

"I was lost. There was nobody for me to talk to about all that you were troubling me with. So I sat alone, with everything inside, and cried myself to sleep."

"I wear my scars proudly. They represent the battles through which I have gone, and I am proud because those battles I have won."

"I went home at night and cried for hours because so many people in my life expecting me to be a certain way was too much pressure, as if I'd been held against a wall and interrogated for hours, asked questions I couldn't quite answer any longer."

"I won't leave a note for anyone to find tomorrow they will know what I've done here tonight."

"I wouldn't be surprised if I was voted most likely to kill everyone at a high school dance."

"I'd rather hang out with the losers that would sit and smoke a cigarette than the ones who wanted to throw a baseball."

"If I would kill myself tonight, who would remember me tomorrow?"

"If you can't solve it, it isn't a problem - its reality. And sometimes reality is the hardest thing to understand and the thing that takes the longest to realize. But once it hits you in the face you'll never forget it. It will always be there in your memories and sometimes that is the best way to look at it."

"If you die you're completely happy and your soul somewhere lives on. I'm not afraid of dying. Total peace after death, becoming someone else is the best hope I've got."

"If you don't like the way I am, then don't come around me. If you don't like the way that I talk, then don't listen. If you don't like the way I dress, then don't look. But don't waste my time telling me about it. I don't care."

"If you forget all else remember just this, there are people who love you and want you happy... without you their life would be empty."

"If you hold back your feelings because you are afraid of getting hurt, you end up hurting anyway."

"I'll fake all the smiles, if it stops all the questions."

"I'm freezing, I'm starving, I'm bleeding to death, everything's fine."

"I'm hurting so bad inside I just wish you could see... I'm struggling to be someone that isn't even close to me."

"I'm just learning how to smile, and that's not easy to

do."

"I'm not afraid of the gun in my hand, I'm not afraid of dying, I'm just afraid of the pain it will bring, and to see my best friends crying."

"I'm not guna give a fuck anymore... If you hurt me, I'm gonna hurt you. That's how it's gonna be from now on..."

"I'm not my usual self being quiet and lonely isn't 'me' crying all night, acting all day this isn't how it's supposed to be."

"I'm often silent when I am screaming inside."

"I'm okay... isn't that what I'm suppose to say?"

"I'm playing a game I can't win, I keep losing and losing, why do I keep playing? To me it isn't about winning or losing, I'm just enjoying the game."

"I'm so broken. Not half full, not half empty, not ever cracked. I'm just broken. I can't exist anymore. I can barely function. There's nothing left to me. And I don't care."

"I'm so happy, cause today I found my friends, they're in my head."

"I'm tired of trying, sick of crying, I know I've been smiling, but inside I'm dying."

"I'm young and I'm hopeless... I'm lost and I know this... I'm going nowhere fast... that's what they say... I'm troublesome, I've fallen... I'm angry at my Father... it's me against this world and I don't care."

"In reality, I'm slowly losing my mind. Underneath the guise of smile, gradually I'm dying inside. Friends ask me how I feel and I lie convincingly. Cause I don't want to reveal the fact that I'm suffering. So I wear my disguise till I go home at night and turn down all the lights and then I break down and cry."

"In that one instance I hated everyone in my life, everyone and everything, and me most of all."

"In the end, music is your only friend."

QUOTES ON DEPRESSION AND SUICIDE

"It is a truth universally acknowledged that the moment one area of your life starts going okay, another part of it falls spectacularly to pieces."

"It requires more courage to suffer than to die."

"It seems to me that the harder I try the harder I fall."

"It was like sawdust, the unhappiness: it infiltrated everything, everything was a problem, everything made her cry - school, homework, boyfriends, the future, the lack of future, the uncertainty of the future, fear of future, fear in general - but it was so hard to say exactly what the problem was in the first place"

"It wasn't a suicide attempt, it was an escape from everything awful. When we cut, we're in control - we make our own pain and we can stop it whenever we want. Physical pain relieves mental anguish. For a brief moment, the pain of cutting is the only thing in the cutter's mind, and when that stops and the other comes back, it is weaker. Drugs do that too, and sex, but not like cutting. Nothing is like cutting."

"It wasn't because I wanted to die, I just wanted the pain to finally stop." -

"It's an interesting feeling, really, to scroll through all the numbers in your phone, and realize that there is no one who will understand."

"It's funny the way you can get use to the tears and the pain."

"It's hard to answer the question "what's wrong" when nothings right."

"It's not how tragically we suffer but how miracously we live."

"I've always been the good girl. The girl whose parents that she would grow up and actually become something. But I'm not like that anymore. I never thought I'd drink or snort those pills but I guess I was wrong. Now that I've done it I don't wanna stop. It's like cutting, once you drag that blade across your skin you can't stop. You don't wanna stop. I know you wanted a perfect teenage girl but in reality there isn't one."

"I've been a loser all my life. I'm not about to change. If you don't like it, there's a door. Nobody made you stay."

"I've come to the point where nothing matters anymore, and things I used to care about aren't worth fighting for."

"I've lived in this place and I know all the faces. Each one is different, but they're always the same. They mean me no harm but it's time that I face it, they'll never allow me to change... But, I never dreamed home would end up where I don't belong... I'm moving on."

"Just because I'm smiling doesn't mean I'm happy."

"Just because some people don't cry, doesn't mean they're not suffering."

"Just when I thought my life was coming together, I realized it was just starting to fall apart."

"Let me give you some advice-- if you are gonna lie about something at least make sure it's worth lying about."

"Let no one think I gave in."

"Let the blood run down your arms then try and tell me everything's okay."

"Life and death are balanced on the edge of a razor."

"Life it seems, will fade away drifting further every day getting lost within myself nothing matters no one else I have lost the will to live simply nothing more to give."

"Loneliness is the human condition. No one is ever going to fill that space."

"Look at me. You may think you see who I really am, but you'll never know me."

"Maybe I am crazy but laughing makes the pain pass by."

"Maybe one day it will be ok again. That's all I want. I don't care what it takes. I just want to be ok again."

"My skin is burnt but it heals my heart, with growing

pride I'll wear my scars, I am honored by you hate."

"My time has come, and so I'm gone. To a better place, far beyond. I love you all as you can see. But it's better now, because I'm free."

"No matter what you do or say, there's nothing that you can do to make people understand you."

"No more joy - No more sadness - No emotion - Only madness. I can't see. I don't feel. I can't touch. I don't heal."

"No one can see the pain what we hide, they're happy for us to keep it inside, our fear is our own; they don't want to know. Why should we involve them; why should it show."

"Not all scars show. Not all wounds heal. Sometimes you can't always see the pain someone feels."

"Nothing can stop me now because I don't care anymore."

"Nothing is more dear to them than their own suffering

- they are afraid that they will lose it - They feel it, like a whip cracking over their heads, striking them and yet befriending them; it wounds them, but it also reassures them."

"On top of feeling sad, I also felt guilty."

"One morning you wake up afraid to live."

"One of the worst feelings in the world is loneliness. Sitting in the dark by yourself in the wee hours of the night gently crying. Nobody knows what's going on with you. How could anybody realize what's happening? Everybody you know is resting peacefully in their bed awaiting the new day tomorrow. But for you, there's no difference in the days. They pass monotonously. And before you know it, it's all gone. "

"Our generation has had no Great war, no Great Depression. Our war is spiritual. Our depression is our lives."

"Our scars have the power to remind us that the past is real."

"Pain is your friend, it tells you when you're seriously injured, it keeps you awake and angry but the best thing about it is it lets you know that you're alive."

"People dislike alcoholics, but they still drink at parties. People sit in nonsmoking section in restaurants, but still enjoy the occasional nicotine jolt. People have strong feelings against self-injurers, but they also take all their emotions out on other people."

"Please don't blame yourself for any of the stupid shit that I choose to do. None of this is your fault. I'm the one who makes these bad decisions so I'm the one who pays the consequences."

"Pull the shades - razor blades - you're so tragic. I hate you so but love you more. I'm so elastic - the things you say - games you play - dirty magic."

"QUIET! I can't hear you & all the voices in my head at the same time!"

"Reality has exiled me; I am no longer bound by its

laws."

"Refuse to feel anything at all, refuse to slip, refuse to fall, can't be weak, can't stand still, watch your back because no one else will."

"Rock bottom is good solid ground, and a dead end street is just a place to turn around."

"Scar tissue has no character. It's not like skin. It doesn't show age or illness or pallor or tan. It has no pores, no hair, no wrinkles. It's like a slip cover. It shields and disguises what's beneath. That's why we grow it; we have something to hide."

"Scars are tattoos with better stories."

"Self-injury is a sign of distress not madness. We should be congratulated on having found a way of surviving."

"She could shut out the whole world, including herself."

"She cuts herself. Never too deep, never enough to die. But enough to feel the pain. Enough to feel the scream inside."

"She is the quietest kind of rebel."

"She was a girl who knew how to be happy even when she was sad and that's important you know."

"She was like a flower that had been battered by a storm, but not quite destroyed. Gradually, she began to strengthen and bloom again."

"She's not the kind of girl who likes to tell the world about the way she feels about herself."

"Skin is beautiful, don't ruin it with scars just because your life isn't as beautiful. For once life becomes beautiful to you again, your skin won't be so beautiful anymore."

"So drop the little razor, and pick up your life, forget all the bad things, the pain and the strife."

"Some of us are just trying to get through the day without falling apart."

"Some people try to understand, but nobody can know what living like this is like."

"Someday I'll fly away."

"Someone once asked me, 'Why do you always insist on taking the hard road?' I replied, 'Why do you assume I see two roads?'"

"Sometimes I feel like no one cares. Sometimes I feel like no one is there. Sometimes I want to kill myself. Sometimes I think I need some help. Sometimes I feel like I'm alone. Sometimes I'm in an empty zone. Sometimes I feel like I'm not alive. Sometimes I wonder if I'm deprived. Sometimes I think the world should end. Sometimes I think I have no friends. Sometimes I want to make them see that sometimes I wish I wasn't me..."

"Sometimes I feel like nobody has held me down and forced me to cry or made me hug them, or seen to the inside of me. I just say 'oh I'm fine' and walk away. Nobody's ever said to me 'no you're not'."

"Sometimes I sit and watch the ink leak from my pen. It

comforts me to know something else bleeds the way I do."

"Sometimes I think that if I wasn't so good at pretending to be, I'd be better at actually being happy."

"Sometimes instead of cutting an X on my wrist I make a cross so that the Lord can forgive me for destroying my body, and I also pray that the pain stops as the blood slowly drips onto my sheets."

"Sometimes it hurts more to smile in front of everyone, then to cry all alone."

"Sometimes it seems like we're all living in some kind of prison, and the crime is how much we all hate ourselves. It's good to get really dressed up once in a while and admit the truth - that when you look closely, people are so strange and complicated that they're actually beautiful. Possibly even me."

"Sometimes the littlest thing in life changes something forever and there will be times when you wish you can go back to how things used to be but you just can't because things have changed so much."

"Sometimes you can cry until there is nothing left wet in you. You can scream and curse to where your throat rebels and ruptures. You can pray all you want to whatever god you think will listen. And still, it makes no difference. It goes on, with no sign as to when it might release you. And you know that if it ever did relent... it would not be because it cared."

"Sometimes you need to run away just to see who will follow you."

"Stop the world I wanna get off."

"Such a pretty girl, happy in an ugly place. Watching all the pretty people do lots of ugly things."

"Take it from someone who's fallen... it's a long way down."

"The apple doesn't fall far from the tree... she's rotten and so beautiful I'd like to keep her here with me and tell her that she's beautiful she takes the pills to fall asleep and dreams that she's invisible tormented dreams she stays awake recalls when she was capable..."

"The beautiful thing about music is when it hits you, you feel no pain."

"The deepest people are the ones who've been hurt the most."

"The drastic steps I'm taking are just an act of desperation, no one's gonna miss me so what the hell. I fought and lied I drank too much. Hurt everyone I ever touched, just how much I hurt you is hard to tell. It's not some kind of cry for help just good bye I wish you well because I love you I'm gonna kill myself."

"The hardest years in life are those between ten and seventy."

"They have no idea what a bottomless pit of misery I am."

"The insane are sane and the sane are insane in a world of craziness."

"The only thing standing between me and total happiness is reality."

"The only thing worse then being hated is being ignored. At least when they hate you they treat you like you exist."

"The pain is there to remind me that I'm still alive."

"The question isn't 'who is going to let me'; it's 'who is going to stop me'."

"The razor moves along her wrist like a river, so peacefully, as that red water starts to escape, its hard to make it stop."

"The skin of a scar is stronger than the original, less aware of pain..."

"The sky isn't always blue. The sun doesn't always shine. So it's okay to fall apart sometimes."

"There is nothing sadder than a child who has barely seen the world, yet who has seen enough of it to know that he does not wish to be a part of it..."

"There is something beautiful about all scars of whatever nature. A scar means the hurt is over, the wound is closed and healed, done with."

"There's a fine line between genius and insanity. I have erased this line."

"There's a girl in my mirror crying tonight and there's nothing I can tell her to make her feel alright..."

"There's a smile on my face but I don't know why it's there... I put it on to satisfy all the people that don't even care."

"There's no excuse for the need to take your own life away, everyone passes through some rough obstacles if life, just face them as they come along, there's always a way to overcome those obstacles, and learn from your experiences."

"There's something about death that is comforting. The thought that you could die tomorrow frees you to appreciate your life now"

"These cuts are leaving creases. Trace the scars, to fit the pieces, to tell your story, you don't need to say a word."

"They say you need to pray, if you want to go to heaven. But they don't tell you what to say when your whole life has gone to hell."

"This isn't a perfect world. People do get hurt. You smile when you feel like crying. You act like you're ok, when you're falling apart inside. And you try to let go, you try to move on, because you know there's nothing else you could do."

"Those feelings that are the most painful are those ones that nobody can explain no quote can describe... and no tears or smiles can make them go away. They're the ones that hurt the deepest the ones that last the longest and take forever to forget about ."

"Those who say sunshine brings happiness have never danced in the rain."

QUOTES ON DEPRESSION AND SUICIDE

"Tired of living and scared of dying."

"To be loved to madness - such was her great desire. Love was to her the one cordial that could drive away the eating loneliness of her days."

"True strength is holding it together when everyone else would understand if you fall apart."

"Unperfect. That's what you can call me. After all I am me, and don't fit a certain category. I'm just a girl who lives life day by day and always manages to put a smile on my face. Even if that day I'm a complete mess."

"We all go a little mad sometimes. Haven't you?"

"Wear a mask that grins and lies, it hides our cheeks and shades our eyes. The debt we pay to human guile, with torn and broken hearts, we smile."

"We're all quite mad here. Ha... ha ha ha ha ha! You may have noticed that I'm not all there myself."

"What do you do when you become too scared, too

scared to live, too scared to die, too scared to love, too scared to even care"

"What you think is what you are. What you peruse becomes your reality."

"What's the point in screaming? No one's listening anyway."

"When I cut myself, I feel so much better. All the little things that might have been annoying me suddenly seem trivial because I'm concentrating on the pain."

"When I was younger crying always seemed to be the answer. Now that I'm older crying seems to be the only option."

"When it seems like everything is wrong and will never be right again remember even the darkest nights must give way to day."

"When you quit fearing pain, when you learn to love the pain, you will lose all fear of everything."

"When you talk about feelings, words were too stiff, they were this and not that, they couldn't include all the meanings. In defining, they always left something out."

"When you're going thru hell... it's best to just keep on going..."

"When you're sure you've had enough of this life... don't let yourself go... because everybody cries... everybody hurts sometimes... sometimes everything is wrong."

"Where ever I am I always find myself looking out the window wishing I was somewhere else."

"Who am I? I am who I say I am and tomorrow someone else entirely."

"Why don't you just sit down, close your eyes and invent your own world? When you were little you did, even with your eyes open."

"Without pain, there would be no suffering, without suffering we would never learn from our mistakes. To make it right, pain and suffering is the key to all windows, without it, there's no way of life."

"Without pain, there would be no suffering, without suffering we would never learn from our mistakes. To make it right, pain and suffering is the key to all windows, without it, there is no way of life."

"You ask why I say nothing's wrong when really everything is. You should know what wrong. You're my friends, your making bad decisions and its killing me to see you suffer like you are. You just never see how what you're doing effects me because you don't care enough to look and see."

"You bleed just to know you're alive."

"You do it to yourself... and that's why it really hurts."

"You have no idea what I can do."

"You know when you cut yourself really badly, it doesn't hurt at all for awhile you don't feel anything - death, our reaction to death is sort of like that you don't feel anything at all and then later on you begin to hurt."

"You look at me and think, 'she's so happy' but there's so much behind this little smile that you will never know."

"You never know when you wake up, if all will be the same, or if you'll be back in your dark place, again to feel the pain."

"You say I'm always happy, and that I'm good at what I do, but what you'll never realize is, I'm a damn good actress too."

"You see her sitting there and you think 'she's so sad' but it's not that she's sad, she's simply given up on pretending to be happy, she's tired of getting up every morning and putting on her fake smile, telling herself 'today will be better'. She doesn't want to be an inconvenience or a bother anymore...she has stopped looking for the light switch in the dark room she calls her life."

"You start life with a clean slate. Then you begin to make your mark. You face decisions, make choices. You keep moving forward. But sooner or later there comes a time where you look back over where you have been and wonder who you really are."

"You're scared because you don't understand... I'm scared because I do."

"...it all becomes completely numbing, like so much pounding on a frozen paralyzed limb that bruises but no longer feels."

ABOUT THE EDITOR

Dr. Krishna N. Sharma born in Muhammadabad Gohana, District Mau, Uttar Pradesh, India on December 24th is an Author, Medical Professional and Educator. He writes articles and columns in various newspapers and magazines of India and Bangladesh. So far he has written and edited 12 books and has made 2 world records.

Contact:
Ph: +91- 9320699167
Email: dr.krisharma@gmail.com
Web: http://www.krishna.info.ms

DR. KRISHNA N. SHARMA (Editor)

CPSIA information can be obtained at www.ICGtesting.com
Printed in the USA
LVOW10s1640210615

443296LV00031B/946/P